30 DEVOTIO
TRUSTI

WHAT'S
THE
HURRY?

publishing team

Director, Student Ministry
Ben Trueblood

Manager, Student Ministry
Publishing
John Paul Basham

Editorial Team Leader
Karen Daniel

Writer
Jennifer Dixon

Content Editor
Kyle Wiltshire

Production Editor
Brooke Hill

Graphic Designer
Kaitlin Redmond

ISBN 978-1-0877-4435-3
Item 005831823
Dewey Decimal Classification Number: 242
Subject Heading: DEVOTIONAL LITERATURE / BIBLE STUDY AND TEACH-ING / GOD

Printed in the United States of America

Student Ministry Publishing
LifeWay Resources
One LifeWay Plaza
Nashville, Tennessee 37234

We believe that the Bible has God for its author; salvation for its end; and truth, without any mixture of error, for its matter and that all Scripture is totally true and trustworthy. To review LifeWay's doctrinal guideline, please visit www.lifeway.com/doctrinalguideline.

Unless otherwise noted, all Scripture quotations are taken from the Christian Standard Bible®, Copyright © 2017 by Holman Bible Publishers. Used by permission. Christian Standard Bible® and CSB® are federally registered trademarks of Holman Bible Publishers.

table of contents

Intro

Your foot bounces furiously. Your fingers drum on your knee. You look at your phone. You look again. You breathe a deep sigh of frustration. Why is it taking so long? It doesn't matter what you're waiting for—your turn in line, the bus to arrive, the update to download—waiting can be challenging. Why does waiting make us so impatient?

As the old saying goes, patience is a virtue. This phrase was actually written almost 800 years ago![1] In those simpler times, what on earth did they have to be patient for? Oddly enough, their world bears some striking similarities to the world we live in today. They had a global pandemic called the Black Plague that swept through the world, gripping everyone in fear. There was a lot of civil unrest between different groups of people as well. They even had technological adances—ironically, most notably the clock—that changed people's lives.[2]

It seems like regardless of what century we're in, no one likes to wait. Why are we all seemingly wired to be impatient? A lot of it is because of our sin nature. So, how can we learn to grow in patience and not be in such a hurry all the time?

Over the next 30 days, we'll explore this question and more. The Bible teaches a lot about patience and has many amazing examples of people God used to do amazing things. Each person had at least one thing in common: they had to wait on God's timing to do the thing that God set them aside to do.

While patience doesn't come naturally, we can learn to grow in this important area of our discipleship journey if we submit ourselves to the Lordship of Jesus and trust Him fully. Impatience is a universal problem, but there is assistance to be found to help us get better at it. You'll see these truths revealed in God's Word as you work your way through this devotional.

getting started

This devotional contains 30 days of content, broken down into sections. Each day is divided into three elements—discover, delight, and display—to help you answer core questions related to Scripture.

discover

This section helps you examine the passage in light of who God is and determine what it says about your identity in relationship to Him. Included here is the daily Scripture reading, focus passage, along with illustrations and commentary to guide you as you explore God's Word.

delight

In this section, you'll be challenged by questions and activities that help you see how God is alive and active in every detail of His Word and your life.

display

Here's where you take action. Display calls you to apply what you've learned through each day's study.

prayer

Each day also includes a prayer activity in one of the three main sections.

Throughout the devotional, you'll also find extra articles and activities to help you connect with the topic personally, such as Scripture memory verses, additional resources, and quotes from leading Christian voices.

day 1

HAND IN HAND

discover |

READ GALATIANS 6:7-10.

Let us not get tired of doing good, for we will reap at the proper time if we don't give up. —Galatians 6:9

We all like to see the rewards of doing a task that requires our time and commitment. If we study for a test, we like to be rewarded with a good grade. If we train for a sport or practice an instrument, we like to see improvement in our ability. Everyone wants to see a good return wherever they invest their time and talents.

When it comes to doing good for others, we may not see benefit for a long time; but Paul tells us "God is not mocked. For whatever a man sows he will also reap" (v.7). In these words, we have assurance that God sees the good we are doing and that He will reward us. He comforts us, explaining that our good deeds are not in vain. Good deeds will be rewarded in the "proper time," which means they are not going to be rewarded in "our time." But we can trust that a time will come when our deeds will be rewarded.

As believers in a good and just God, we have the assurance that God will make use of the good we do. So, we should continue working for the good of others even when we are tempted to stop because we are seeing so little come from it. We know our rewards are from God and not from what we can see. We also know that doing good for others and being patient often go hand in hand.

delight |

When do you get discouraged from doing good? Where does your discouragement come from?

How does God's promise that He will reward the good you do encourage you to be patient with the process?

display |

Think of the last time you quit or were tempted to quit doing good for someone because you got discouraged. Journal the reasons why you did not want to do good in that situation and write down a different course of action instead of abandoning what is right. Memorize Galatians 6:9 as well, as a reminder to persevere when doing good grows difficult.

> Thank God that no act of good goes unnoticed by Him. Tell Him about when you get discouraged and why you want to stop doing good for others at times. Ask for His help to remain faithful and patient to keep doing good even when you want to quit.

day 2

REMAINING HOPEFUL

discover |

READ ROMANS 8:18-25.

Now if we hope for what we do not see, we eagerly wait for it with patience.
—Romans 8:25

We all have a sense deep down inside us that this world is not what it should be. What is a person to do with the disappointment that comes with living in this not-so-perfect world? Some people chose to stop hoping. They choose to look inward and live for the right now and only for themselves. Other people shut the world out; they assume that by not interacting with others they can avoid being hurt. Still others choose not to trust anyone else. These people essentially place themselves as "god" of their own destiny.

The apostle Paul challenged us in Romans 8 to not give up hope and instead to "eagerly wait for it with patience." Hope is a desire for a certain thing to happen and requires trust in someone or something apart from one's self. When you hope, you acknowledge that you can give your very best, but the outcome is still not totally up to you.

In this world, it is impossible to be patient without hope. For us to wait patiently, we have to hold on to the hope that the outcome will be better than the present moment. As Christians, our hope is founded in our trust in a good, just, and faithful God. When hope seems to falter, look to strengthen your trust in God.

delight |

Recall a time you were truly disappointed in your circumstances or in someone else. How did a lack of hope play a part in your thoughts and behavior?

How would a belief in someone bigger than yourself who is in control of the future change your outlook on that disappointment?

display |

Carefully read Romans 8:31-39. Do you realize how much God loves you? Whenever your hope seems to be fading, read these verses to remind you that you can trust Him. Your beliefs in God will directly impact your trust in Him and, consequently, your ability to remain hopeful.

> Acknowledge your disappointments to God. Tell Him what you are deeply longing for, but maybe aren't getting at the moment. Ask Him to help strengthen your trust in Him when you are impatient for things to be different.

day 3

LOVE IS PATIENT

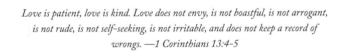

discover|

READ 1 CORINTHIANS 13:1-5.

Love is patient, love is kind. Love does not envy, is not boastful, is not arrogant, is not rude, is not self-seeking, is not irritable, and does not keep a record of wrongs. —1 Corinthians 13:4-5

I don't know about you, but the way love is described here is exactly what I would want in a best friend. Who doesn't want a friend that is patient, kind, does not envy, does not boast, and is not arrogant or rude? Someone who is not all about themselves and is not irritable and does not hold onto past wrongs? That friend sounds amazing!

Jesus said that "whatever you want others to do for you, do also the same for them" (Matt. 7:25). Jesus (who is also God, by the way) thought it was important enough to say this commandment sums up the Law and the Prophets. In other words, this simple commandment is a summary of what God wanted His people to do and what the Prophets called the people to return to doing!

We are all a work in progress. We all need to show patience and have others be patient with us. Irritation and frustration will inevitably arise in your relationships, but in those moments, remember how wonderful it is when someone shows you patience.

"Love is patient." It is so very telling that when the apostle Paul (inspired by the Holy Spirit) wrote out a definition of love, the first word he chose to describe love was "patient." Patience is key to showing love to others and feeling loved by others.

delight |

Think about how you like to be treated by others. What difference does patience make in how you like others to treat you?

How do you respond to others when they become irritable and easily angered? How can you show patience to them in those moments?

display |

It is inevitable—you will become impatient with someone else this week (maybe even today). Consider how you can be more patient with that person. Practice speaking a quick prayer of "Lord help me be patient right now" before you respond to that person. If it is someone you have an exceptionally hard time showing love to, talk to a trusted adult about your difficulties. Listen as they share their experiences. Everyone struggles in this area, but it doesn't mean you should stop trying to show patience to others.

> Confess to God your impatience to others and when you don't love others as you should. Ask the Holy Spirit within you to help you love others. If there is someone in particular you have a hard time loving, pray for that person and ask God to teach you to love him or her.

day 4

GOD'S CALLED PEOPLE

discover|

READ EPHESIANS 4:1-6.

Therefore I, the prisoner in the Lord, urge you to walk worthy of the calling you have received, with all humility and gentleness, with patience, bearing with one another in love, making every effort to keep the unity of the Spirit through the bond of peace. —Ephesians 4:1-3

Consider this line from today's Scripture reading: "walk worthy of the calling you have received." What is this "calling"? If you look back at Ephesians 1:5, the apostle Paul says "God predestined us to be adopted as sons through Jesus Christ." If you trust in Jesus, God has called you into His family!

You did nothing to earn this position. It was given freely to you by the death and resurrection of Jesus, yet God calls you to live in a way that is worthy of this high calling. These verses lay out for you what it looks like to be worthy of the designation as a child of God.

Humility, gentleness, patience, bearing with one another in love, and staying united in peace are qualities of someone worthy to be called a child of God. These qualities reflect to the world around you the kind of God you serve.

When you choose to have patience with others, you are showing that you have a higher calling given to you by your Heavenly Father. You are showing others that they are important enough to wait on. Hopefully, one day you'll get to share with them that God thinks they are important as well.

delight |

Have you ever considered being patient as part of a higher calling from God? How does that change your outlook on showing patience to others?

Take a moment to consider God's character in light of the fact that He desires His followers to be patient. Since God wants His children to be patient, what does that say about Him?

display |

Now that you know being patient with others is part of a higher calling from God, imagine those moments when you lose patience. Consider the thoughts that run through your head as you are growing impatient, irritable, and angry. Journal one way you will combat those thoughts with the thought that you have a higher calling than what is going on right at that moment.

Praise God that you don't have to meet a standard to be called one of His children. Thank Him for the sacrifice of Jesus on your behalf. Pray that God will continue to add the qualities He finds worthy in His children to you.

day 5

PRIDE VS. PATIENCE

discover |

READ ECCELESIATES 7:8B-9.

A patient spirit is better than a proud spirit. Don't let your spirit rush to be angry, for anger abides in the hearts of fools.

The book of Eccelesiates was written by the wisest king ever to live—Solomon. In this book, he laid out what he discovered about living life well. He pointed out that so much of what we invest our time and energy in is not eternal. Solomon wrote that pride was a character trait of fools. To be prideful is to consider yourself more important than others; it's a desire to protect self rather than follow God's plan. Those who choose to continue to follow this path and reject God's instructions were called fools (Ps. 14:1). A fool doesn't trust a good and sovereign God; they only trust themselves.

Notice also that Solomon also wrote not to "let your spirit rush to be angry." Rushing to anger is describing exactly how a proud person responds to conflict. A proud person wants to control, but a wise person wants to understand. A wise person is patient. He or she asks questions, tries to assess the situation from different viewpoints, and considers ways that will lead to the benefit of all who are involved in the conflict.

Solomon was a king who had it all—wealth, power, influence, and love. Yet his advice about living the good life is attainable for everyone: "A patient spirit is better than a proud spirit." It is astounding how such simple advice helps us so greatly toward living a satisfying life.

delight |

Read through Proverbs 15 and write down any observations you make on how to handle an argument with wisdom.

Consider your own life. Do you want to be a person who trusts in God or someone who thinks they have all the answers without seeking knowledge elsewhere? What do your actions say about who you are trusting?

display |

When you feel anger about to overcome you, stop. Consider how you can show patience to yourself or someone else. Try asking a question to gain understanding about the situation instead of assuming you know exactly what is going on. Write out a scenario where you can patiently pause and ask a clarifying question rather than pridefully assuming you understand and responding in anger.

Pray that the Lord will show you your pride. Ask Him to humble you and to teach you patience. Confess any personal areas or people in your life you struggle to be patient with.

What Makes Me Impatient?

We all have our moments of impatience, whether we let our attitude show or not. Take a look at the following list and mark how impatient you would feel in this situation.

1 = "This is great!"
5 = "This is annoying, but I can handle it."
10 = "Why me?"

A younger friend, sibling, or neighbor keeps asking me questions, following me around, or copying everything I say and do.

1   2   3   4   5   6   7   8   9   10

My best friend hasn't responded to the text I sent three days ago!

1   2   3   4   5   6   7   8   9   10

I worked really hard on a class project, but I'm worried I didn't do it correctly, and it hasn't been graded yet.

1   2   3   4   5   6   7   8   9   10

I can't wait until I'm able to stay home by myself/drive/stay out later/other.

1   2   3   4   5   6   7   8   9   10

The person in front of me at the restaurant took a long time to decide what they wanted, then ordered several things. I feel like I've been waiting forever!

1   2   3   4   5   6   7   8   9   10

It seems everything is instant these days. The problem with an instant society is that not everything is *actually* instant, and that makes us impatient. But impatience is more than a negative attitude—it isn't healthy. Here's the thing: patience isn't just good for your physical and mental health, it's also biblical. God is fully aware of our humanity—He created us! He knew we would have our impatient moments, and He provided plenty of instruction for us about being patient in all things and with all people.

But how do we cultivate patience—especially for those difficult moments when we'd rather scream or sigh dramatically because we're still waiting?

Here are four key verses about cultivating patience in your life. Write out each of these verses on a note card and read one of them the next time you feel impatient. At the very least, it'll give you something to do while you wait. But the important thing is that you'll be learning to hide God's Word in your heart—the key to responding to any difficult situation (Ps. 119:11).

Patience is better than power,
and controlling one's emotions, than capturing a city.
—Proverbs 16:32

Now may the God who gives endurance and encouragement grant you to live in harmony with one another, according to Christ Jesus.
—Romans 15:5

Let us not get tired of doing good, for we will reap at
the proper time if we don't give up.
—Galatians 6:9

My dear brothers and sisters, understand this: Everyone should be quick to listen, slow to speak, and slow to anger, for human anger does not accomplish God's righteousness.
—James 1:19-20

day 6

PATIENT WITH EVERYONE

---

discover|

READ 1 THESSALONIANS 5:12-21.

And we exhort you, brothers and sisters: warn those who are idle, comfort the discouraged, help the weak, be patient with everyone. —1 Thessalonians 5:14

In this letter to the church in Thessalonica, the apostle Paul pleaded with the people to live a life that revealed what freedom in Christ looked like. He compared not knowing the grace and mercy of Jesus to being "asleep" or being in the dark. He compared knowing and experiencing that grace as being "awake" or in the light (1 Thess. 5:5-8).

Paul gave several instructions on what life looks like when people are "awake" and living in the light. He described a community of people who respect those who work hard, encourage one another, comfort each other, help those that are weak, and are patient with everyone. Could you imagine living with people who lived this way!? What an impact this community of people would have!

Notice that Paul identified the recipients of each specific command: We are to warn the idle, comfort the discouraged, help the weak, and be patient with everyone. The instruction to be patient is to be given to *everyone*. Being patient is a part of being "awake"— a part of experiencing and knowing the love, grace, and mercy of Jesus. To be patient is a gift God allows us to utilize when we've experienced and known the patience of Jesus. We are free to let go of our controlling, impatient, and unhealthy patterns of life to be patient with others instead.

---

delight |

Do you think knowing the love of Jesus is freeing? Why or why not?

Consider how your life would be different if you saw God's command to be patient as a privilege and not a burden. What is one example of how things might be different for you if you thought this way?

display |

Are there some people who you find it easier to be patient with than others? This week, take notice of who you show patience to and who you don't. Try to understand your responses to these people and talk with God about helping you find patience for everyone you encounter. Write down the name of one person you need extra patience with and ask God to grant it to you.

Ask God to help you see patience as a gift from Him and not a burden. Ask Him to keep you in His grace and to continue the work of making you more like His Son Jesus.

CHARACTER BUILDING

discover |

READ ROMANS 5:1-5.

And not only that, but we also rejoice in our afflictions, because we know that affliction produces endurance, endurance produces proven character, and proven character produces hope. This hope will not disappoint us, because God's love has been poured out in our hearts through the Holy Spirit who was given to us.
—Romans 5:3-5

What an odd thing for the apostle Paul to write to Christians in Rome: "We also rejoice in our afflictions." No one ever associates rejoicing with afflictions. Pain, suffering, and difficulties come with affliction—and none of those are reasons for rejoicing. Why should we rejoice in afflictions?

The apostle Paul said the affliction itself isn't what leads us to rejoice, but what is happening to us *through* the affliction. Affliction produces character. Character is our inner strength to maintain our values and principles, even when it's tough. God wants you to have character. He wants you to be able to maintain what's most important when circumstances look bleak. This character produced in you as you endure tough things brings hope.

Hope is an amazing quality. People who are able to hope can cope so much better in life. Christians can hope with confidence that our God has conquered even our worst fears when He demonstrated victory over death. Christians have a different, enduring kind of hope because we follow a God who lives, and we know death is not the end.

delight |

How do you tend to respond to the difficulties* in your life? Do you typically endure patiently?

What's one way you can patiently endure through a difficulty you may be facing today? How can you maintain hope?

display |

Do your own personal research on hope. Search the internet for the benefits of hope. Talk to successful people and ask them what role hope played in their philosophy on life. Record your findings in your journal and start to implement hopeful thinking today.

> Ask the Lord to be with you in your afflictions. Tell Him all your troubles. He cares for you (1 Pet. 5:7). Pray for His strength to help you endure.

*You may want to talk to a parent, pastor or another trusted adult about your difficulties. God never said we are to endure alone. Some afflictions can be addressed by talking to someone in authority about what is going on.

day 8

THE LORD IS COMING

discover |

READ JAMES 5:7-8.

Therefore, brothers and sisters, be patient until the Lord's coming. See how the farmer waits for the precious fruit of the earth and is patient with it until it receives the early and the late rains. You also must be patient. Strengthen your hearts, because the Lord's coming is near.

James, the brother of Jesus and early church leader, wrote these words to Jewish Christians who were spread throughout the world due to persecution (Acts 8:1). James wrote to people whose lives were in danger and couldn't return home. If anyone needed encouragement, it was James' audience. James told them to "be patient until the Lord's coming." He knew this promise ofJesus' return was their greatest hope in dark times.

What are the signs of Jesus' return? They aren't exactly "good": anguish on the earth, people overwhelmed with fear, and people having to flee their homes (Luke 21:20-22). Looking back, we can see the impact this scattering of people from Jerusalem had on the world: the good news of Jesus Christ made its way to others that weren't in Jerusalem.

It was through this scattering that many were introduced to Jesus for the first time—all because the people who were scattered didn't give up hope. They patiently waited for the Lord to return. They told others about Him and His promises. Today, He is still working miracles for many to come to faith in Him before He makes His final return.

delight |

Have you ever felt abandoned by Jesus and all on your own? What thoughts did you experience? How did you deal with those thoughts and feelings?

Pay attention to your surroundings—your home, family, friends, opportunities, etc. What are some signs in your life that He might be blessing you right now?

display |

Take some time to observe nature. Marvel at the sun, moon, and stars. Watch the insects as they build or work. Touch the morning dew on a plant and smell a flower. Nature is a great way to see God has not abandoned us.

> Thank God for the beauty of His creation as a reminder He is still at work. Tell Him when you feel like He has abandoned you and ask Him to remind you of His presence daily.

day 9

HE HEARS

discover |

READ PSALM 40:1-3.

I waited patiently for the Lord, and he turned to me and heard my cry for help. He brought me up from the desolate pit, out of the muddy clay, and set my feet on a rock, making my steps secure. He put a new song in my mouth, a hymn of praise to our God. Many will see and fear, and they will trust in the Lord.

Do you ever picture patient people as those who don't say anything and can sit quietly with hands folded in their laps for a long time? Psalm 40 gives us a different picture of patience. This Psalm was written by David, who was recalling a time when he was in a difficult situation. He described this time as being in a "desolate pit."

David did not sit down in his pit and quietly wait for someone to help him out. He cried out for help! His waiting patiently involved prayer—fervent, meaningful, genuine, raw, and pleading prayer. God heard and delivered him. David wrote, "He put a new song in my mouth, a hymn of praise." It would seem that David's song prior to being rescued wasn't a song of praise. It might've been one of confession, groaning, and sorrow.

Let David, a man after God's own heart, shake any preconceived notions you may have about being patient. Being patient isn't always sunshine and rainbows. Being patient is clinging to God as if there is no other way out of your mess. It is crying to Him, telling Him what is wrong, and asking Him to do something.

delight |

Is David's description in Psalm 40 what you would consider patient? Why or why not?

How has reading Psalm 40 changed your idea of what patience looks like?

display |

Biblical patience is not denial of the need for a Savior. It is not distracting ourselves with things of this world until Jesus comes back. It is fervently seeking God for our problems right now. God is big enough to take on your groanings. He wants to help you if you will just seek Him out.

Read Jesus' parable on prayer in Luke 18:1-8 and consider how you could be more persistent in your prayer life. Write out one idea of how to grow in your prayer life and act on it.

> Start talking to God about your struggles. Push aside any preconceived ideas that "He doesn't want to hear my complaining" or "He has more important things to do than listen to me." Just open up to Him about what it is you are going through and ask for His help.

day 10

REMOVING HINDRANCES

discover|

READ HEBREWS 12:1-2.

Therefore, since we also have such a large cloud of witnesses surrounding us, let us lay aside every hindrance and the sin that so easily ensnares us. Let us run with endurance the race that lies before us, keeping our eyes on Jesus, the source and perfecter of our faith. For the joy that lay before him, he endured the cross, despising the shame, and sat down at the right hand of the throne of God.

Trusting in God's promises, acting in obedience to Him, and then patiently waiting for your reward is not easy. The men and women in the Bible who are applauded for their faith clung to God no matter what. They continued believing God even when it meant facing catastrophic floods, leaving family and home, rejecting riches and power, and fighting seemingly impossible battles. The author of Hebrews compared this waiting to an endurance race.

Enduring the pain of a long race takes effort. Yes, God will help you and see you through, but you are not a passive participant in the journey of faith. If you want to run well, you must throw off anything that hinders you and remain faithful. The Bible provides lists of sins and stumbling blocks for people as well as stories of people who have fallen, but you must examine your own life to learn what is hindering your faith and take action to remove it from your life.

Most importantly, you are to keep your focus on Jesus. Remember His promises of eternal and abundant life, to be with you and never forsake you, and to bring you into the family of God. These are your rewards for the taking if you will remain patient and faithful.

delight |

What are some hindrances that might keep you from remaining faithful to God?

Look up John 3:16; 10:10; 14:27; and Ephesians 1:5. What are the rewards given to Jesus' followers if they remain faithful to Him?

display |

Take action against something hindering your faithfulness to God. If you feel stuck or helpless, talk to another trusted Christian or pastor for help. Don't expect big changes overnight, but consider one small step you can make right now and write it below.

Praise God for His promise of rewards. Ask Him to motivate your heart to remain faithful and to work to move aside all hindrances.

Let us not get tired of doing good,

for we will reap at the proper time if we don't give up.

day 11

WAITING ON OTHERS

discover|

READ 2 PETER 3:9.

The Lord does not delay His promise, as some understand delay, but is patient with you, not wanting any to perish but all to come to repentance.

The apostle Peter wrote this letter to encourage believers in their faith. In chapters 2 and 3, Peter talked about people who spread lies in an attempt to turn believers away from their faith. He said that these people will reject God and tell His followers that He is not coming back. Peter warned people to not believe these lies.

He told them to look at creation instead. He said that people who reject God forget the world He created and how it all came to be. The apostle Paul even said God's "eternal power and divine nature have been clearly seen since the creation of the world" (Rom. 1:20). These "scoffers," as Peter called them, ignore God's displays of glory, question His existence, and encourage people to doubt whether Jesus will really come back to save them (2 Pet. 3:3-4).

Jesus has good reason for "delaying" His return. He is being patient for all to come to Him—He will wait for His people to repent. His "delaying" is not to discourage you, but to allow others to come to Him in faith.

As Peter said, "With the Lord one day is like a thousand years, and a thousand years like one day" (2 Pet. 1:8). For many of us, patience wanes when something is taking longer than we'd like. For God, time is not that way. He has the patience to wait for even the most wicked of us to realize our need for Him.

delight |

When do you find yourself growing impatient with God?

Why might it be easier to wait when you know Jesus has a purpose behind His waiting?

display |

Examine your faith. Do you truly trust that God is good and that Jesus will return? If you have doubts, talk to God about them. Seek out some older and wiser Christians and ask them what doubts they have had and how they have dealt with them. Write one doubt you struggle with and seek out a trusted adult to discuss this doubt with.

Praise God that he wants good for all. Acknowledge His goodness. Pray for God to secure your faith in Him even when others may question it.

day 12

ALL GLORY TO HIM

discover |

READ 1 TIMOTHY 1:12-17.

But I received mercy for this reason, so that in me, the worst of them, Christ Jesus might demonstrate his extraordinary patience as an example to those who would believe in Him for eternal life. Now to the King eternal, immortal, invisible, the only God, be honor and glory forever and ever. Amen. —1 Timothy 1:16-17

The great apostle Paul—who wrote most of the New Testament—had a dark past. He was once a persecutor of the church. He invaded people's homes, arrested them, and dragged them off to prison if he found out they followed Jesus. (According to Acts 8:3, he was known as Saul at the time he was persecuting Christians.) Christians were terrified of Paul. For this reason, he called himself "a blasphemer, a persecutor, and an arrogant man" (1 Tim. 1:13).

But something amazing happened to Paul: Jesus appeared to him in a blinding light and gave him a chance to stop his wicked ways and begin to follow God (Acts 9). Paul described his salvation as a gift of mercy from Jesus. He said Jesus displayed "extraordinary patience" with him.

Paul is not unique in God's patient offering of salvation. It is offered to all who will follow Jesus. Salvation is not based on anything you have done or will do, but on the patient, merciful nature of God. When we see our salvation through this lens, we can't help but offer praise to the God who has been so good to us.

delight |

Has your understanding of salvation been that it is all about your doing, or do you understand the mercy and patience of God on your behalf? Explain.

How can you give glory to God for your salvation?

display |

Take time to ponder one of the ways you can show glory to God: maybe talk with someone about God's impact on your life, sing a song of praise, or consider how you can serve others. Commit to doing that action this week. Write below how you'll give God glory for His patience with you.

> Praise God for who He is, what He has done, and what He has promised to do in the future. Confess times when you haven't praised Him as you should, and ask for His help to acknowledge His patience with you.

day 13

SLOW TO ANGER

discover |

READ PSALM 103:8-13.

The Lord is compassionate and gracious, slow to anger and abounding in faithful love. —Psalm 103:8

The great King David of Israel wrote, "The Lord is slow to anger and abounding in faithful love." But David is certainly not the first or only person in the Bible to make this claim about God. God is the first one recorded as making this claim about Himself. As Moses went on Mount Sinai to receive the Ten Commandments, God said these words about Himself: "The Lord is a compassionate and gracious God, slow to anger and abounding in faithful love and truth" (Ex. 34:6).

It is astounding that the God who created the world and everything in it, who has all power, who can be anywhere at any time, and who knows everything, would choose "slow to anger and abounding in faithful love" as the way to describe Himself! It is because these are the qualities of His nature He wants you to know about foremost. It is important to God that you understand His nature—that whatever He does, He is slow to anger and abounding in faithful love.

Notice in the verses that follow David wrote about God's willingness to forgive and remove the sins of those who fear Him. His patience with His people is a demonstration of His faithful love to them. David compared God to a father showing compassion to his children. God wants us to know that His nature is one that is patient and loving.

delight |

What words would you use to describe God's nature?

Why do you think God chose—out of all His attributes—to say He was "slow to anger and abounding in faithful love"?

display |

Consider God's loving kindness to you. Decide how you can share that loving kindness with someone else. Write out his or her name and one way you can be patient and slow to anger when you interact with him or her.

Thank God for His loving nature. Thank Him for His forgiveness of sins, abounding love, and relenting anger. Praise Jesus for taking the punishment of your sin on the cross so that you can be in a right relationship with God the Father.

day 14

discover |

READ PSALM 30:5.

For His anger only lasts a moment, but His favor, a lifetime. Weeping may stay overnight, but there is joy in the morning.

King David, who wrote Psalm 30, was called "a man after [God's] own heart" (1 Sam. 13:14). He understood God's nature and exemplified it throughout his life; however, David was far from perfect. He made some atrocious mistakes. He had an affair with a married woman and had her husband murdered. His family life was a wreck as well. He had multiple wives and a son who had another one of David's sons killed.

David knew about God's anger. He faced several harsh consequences for his disobedience. However, we see David repent throughout his life when confronted with his sins. In Psalm 51, he prayed fervently for God not to leave him and to forgive him.

God forgave David and blessed him with a son, Solomon. God would establish an eternal kingdom through Solomon's descendant, Jesus (2 Sam. 7:11-13). David experienced both the anger of God and the favor of God. He understood that God does not tolerate wickedness, but is willing to forgive all who genuinely repent.

His anger is momentary, but His favor is for a lifetime. God's anger toward sin is real. If it wasn't, then Jesus didn't need to die on the cross. But His favor is so much greater than His anger. His anger will be satisfied and will come to an end, but His steadfast love for His people will never stop.

delight |

Have you ever felt like God was too angry at you to forgive you? Why or why not?

Read Romans 8:31-39. What is your assurance that the love of God will never run out for you?

display |

Morning represents a new start. This morning (if you are doing this devotion in the morning) or tomorrow morning (if you are doing this in the afternoon or evening), write a journal entry about how grateful you are to receive His forgiveness. Ask Him to help you genuinely repent of sins and to get a fresh start. Ask Him to turn places of weeping in your life to joy.

> Rejoice that God's anger is momentary, but His favor is for a lifetime. If you feel God is angry with you, then confess your sin to Him and plead for Him to remove it from you. Place your trust in Jesus' work on the cross on your behalf.

day 15

BEING PATIENT THROUGH DISCIPLINE

discover |

READ LAMENTATIONS 3:22-33.

The Lord is good to those who wait for him, to the person who seeks him. It is good to wait quietly for salvation from the Lord. —Lamentations 3:25-26

Lamentations is a book written about the destruction of the city of Jerusalem. God warned the people this destruction was coming. They had been told multiple times that if they didn't turn from their wickedness, disaster was coming (Jer. 18:11-12). God eventually did not protect them from the destruction of their holy city when the Babylonians attacked (Lam. 2:17). The city was destroyed, many were killed, and peoples lives were left in utter ruin.

The hardship that followed the devastation was intense. Families were dying and people were going to extreme measures to provide for themselves. All these tragedies surrounding the writer of Lamentations made his words more inspiring. He knew that this discipline from the Lord would not last forever.

He was able to remain patient by reminding himself of God's goodness: "The steadfast love of the Lord never ceases" (v. 22). He understood God's desire was not to punish His people, but to redeem them. He saw this discipline as an invitation to draw near to God. Eventually, God brought salvation to His people and not just to Judah, but to all who place their trust in Him (John 3:16-17).

delight |

Imagine for a moment if you were never disciplined. How would you behave if there were no consequences for your actions?

Read Hebrews 12:3-13. What do you learn about God's purpose for discipline?

display |

We can not assume that every bad situation we encounter is God disciplining us for some sin we have committed in the past. Sometimes bad things happen to us because people are bad or because we live in a world where natural disasters happen. Whatever the cause, it is important to remember God cares for you. Talk to Him when you are confused about why something horrible may be happening to you or someone you love and remind yourself of His goodness. Memorize Lamentations 3:25-26 to help you remember God's goodness even during difficult times.

Thank God that He cares enough for you to discipline you. Ask Him to help you remain faithful when you are going through tough situations.

day 16

GOD HAS A PLAN

━━━━━━━━

discover |

READ JEREMIAH 29:10-14.

"For I know the plans I have for you"—this is the Lord's declaration—"plans for your well-being, not for disaster, to give you a future and a hope."
—Jeremiah 29:11

The nation of Babylon conquered Jerusalem. They deported the people and forced them to live in a foreign land. But God gave a word to the prophet Jeremiah to give the people instruction and encouragement. God told them to continue living where they were. He told them to build homes, work, farm, get married, and grow families in Babylon (Jer. 29:4-7). He told them to seek good for the city where He placed them, even if it was not their home. He had a plan for them that might not be what they imagined, but was certainly for their benefit. His plan for their lives didn't include them hanging on to the past or wishing for how things used to be.

Where you are right now may not be where you want to be. Maybe all the conditions in your life aren't ideal, but God wants you to flourish. So, how are you to flourish in the meantime? God has a plan for you. His plan for you is to live out His kingdom in your life.

Jesus told us some ways to flourish in Matthew 5. He told us to be peacemakers, to be pure in heart, and to seek after righteousness. He told us to work out our anger with others, to not let our lust control our actions, and to remain committed in our relationships. It may seem simplistic, but these instructions are how we flourish until Jesus returns. It is His plan, and in the end, He will work it out for good.

delight |

Do you feel like you are not where you want to be in your life right now? How is that affecting your thoughts and behaviors?

How can knowing that God has a plan for your future be helpful in remaining patient when things aren't perfect?

display |

Decide to stop wallowing in self-pity. Consider one small step you can take to flourish where you are. Think of something that would serve and build relationships with others. Once you take that first step, the others follow more easily. Write down one idea below.

Thank God that He has a good plan for you. Praise Him that He is on your side and doing things for your good. Confess times when you felt forgotten and ask Him to remind you of His presence when you feel like you've been left behind.

The Lord is good to those who wait for him, to the person who seeks him. It is good to wait quietly for salvation from the Lord.

LAMENTATIONS 3:25-26

day 17

HIS WAYS ARE NOT MINE

discover |

READ ISAIAH 55:6-9.

"For my thoughts are not your thoughts, and your ways are not my ways." This is the Lord's declaration. "For as heaven is higher than earth, so my ways are higher than your ways, and my thoughts than your thoughts." —Isaiah 55:8-9

Like Jeremiah, the prophet Isaiah wrote to the people of Judah who had been displaced from their homes and were now residing in Babylon. They were devastated by what happened to their nation and were discouraged about having to settle down in Babylon. But God wanted them to know that all was not lost. He invited them to come to Him.

In Isaiah 55, God told the people not to pursue things that don't satisfy. Instead, He told the people to come to Him for satisfaction. He called them to seek Him and to stop their wickedness, and He promised that He would forgive them. He reminded them that He was unlike them. He thinks and acts differently than they would anticipate.

God is not always predictable. His nature is immutable—meaning it'll never change. God will always be loving and just, but you will not always be able to predict His patterns. We will probably be confused at times about what God is doing and what He is accomplishing. This confusion is because God is working a whole universe for His glory and our good. It's not always going to make sense to us in the moment, but we can rest assured He is in control and has a plan that is greater than we could ever imagine.

delight |

In what areas of your life do you fall into the trap of looking for satisfaction apart from God?

How does it comfort you to know that God is unlike you in His thoughts and actions?

display |

Spend some time examining where you are putting your satisfaction. It may be a relationship, a hobby, or an identity you have adopted. Ask yourself: *Is it sinful to continue after this thing*? If yes, then take action to stop pursuing it. If not, ask: *How can I put this thing in priority below God*?

Confess when you have not sought God for your satisfaction and have pursued other things. Thank God that He is not like you. He does not worry or fret, but He is confident in His plan.

day 18

A STRAIGHT PATH

discover |

READ PROVERBS 3:5-6.

Trust in the Lord with all your heart, and do not rely on your own understanding; in all your ways know him, and he will make your paths straight.

This proverb was written from a father, King Solomon, to his son. The father told his son how to have a prosperous life that's full of joy. His instructions were for the good of his son and to help his son avoid common pitfalls many others fell into. If he followed the instructions, he would have favor with men and God.

Solomon said to trust the Lord with *all* of one's heart. He didn't give allowance for any half-way trusting. Life-giving trust in God is whole-hearted trust. Jesus said something similar in Matthew 22:37: "to love the Lord your God with all your heart." Jesus called it the greatest commandment. In fact, Jesus said all of the Law God has given stems from this central commandment, along with loving others as ourselves (Matt. 22:40). Needless to say, this one action of whole-hearted trust in God embodies just about everything God has for us to do.

Your teenage years can feel like times of tumultuous waiting for your "real life" to begin. You have so many important decisions to make in the upcoming years that will chart the course for the rest of your life. No matter the course you choose, you can't go wrong if you are trusting in God with all your heart. Seek Him for wisdom and make decisions based on what you understand to be the most God-honoring choice.

delight |

Who do you turn to for help on tough decisions?

Have you ever made decisions merely based on what everyone else around you is doing? How did that decision turn out?

display |

Consider a big decision you have to make in the near future. Write down what wisdom you have gained from God's Word that might pertain to the decision. Talk to people you trust who are faithfully following Jesus and ask them what insight they might bring to this decision.

Talk to God about the decisions that are weighing on you. Ask for His wisdom in those situations. Thank Him for giving you His Word the Bible and the church for insight on how to find wisdom outside yourself.

day 19

LIFE'S INTERRUPTIONS

discover |

READ ACTS 16:6-10.

After he had seen the vision, we immediately made efforts to set out for Macedonia, concluding that God had called us to preach the gospel to them.
—Acts 16:10

The book of Acts was written by a doctor turned missionary named Luke. He described a particular journey in Acts 16 where Paul was prohibited by God from entering a certain location. Paul was not one to shy away from difficult circumstances. He continued to preach in places where he knew he could be persecuted and possibly murdered (Acts 14:19-20). So, Paul wasn't making excuses by saying the Holy Spirit forbid them to go there.

After being told not to go to Asia or Bithynia, Paul received a dream that led him to go to Macedonia. Apparently Macedonia was not where Paul planned to go next, but God had other plans. It would seem that bringing the good news of Jesus would be good for any location, so why was God so forceful about going to Macedonia? Sometimes God throws a detour in what seems to be a good path. Remember, His ways are not our ways. But Paul remained faithful wherever he went, and we should do the same.

Unplanned turns will happen on everyone's journey in life. It is what we do when those turns happen that really matters. Don't let detours throw you off God's plan to bring about His kingdom wherever you go and through whatever you are doing. Remain patient and trust in Him.

delight |

Has God stopped an opportunity or a relationship from happening that you felt so sure would work out great? How did you react?

What might you be missing out on when you choose your own way instead of God's way?

display |

C.S. Lewis once wrote, "The great thing, if one can, is to stop regarding all the unpleasant things in life as interruptions of one's 'own', or 'real' life. The truth is of course that what one calls interruptions are precisely one's real life—the life God is sending one day by day: what one calls one's 'real life' is a phantom of one's own imagination."[3] Read over this quote slowly and multiple times. Decide today to let the interruptions that come your way be welcomed as God's way of giving you a new opportunity.

> Tell God about the times you've been disappointed by plans that have failed. Ask Him to renew your confidence that He has not abandoned you. Pray for Him to continue to guide your steps for your good and His glory, even if it is painful.

day 20

IT'S NOT ALWAYS ABOUT YOU

discover |

READ ACTS 16:11-15.

A God-fearing woman named Lydia, a dealer in purple cloth from the city of Thyatira, was listening. The Lord opened her heart to respond to what Paul was saying. —Acts 16:14

After God interrupted Paul's plans for travel, Paul ended up in a town called Philippi. In his time there, he sought out people who were already seeking after God. He wanted to tell them about Jesus. Remember, Jesus had only been crucified and resurrected 40 years prior, and news did not spread as fast as it does today. Paul's traveling to those places brought life-changing information. His words gave direction and meaning to their entire lives.

One such person was Lydia. Notice that the Bible described her as "a God-fearing woman." Lydia believed in God and was looking to know Him better. Paul's words gave her that fulfillment. Her faith in Jesus even spread to everyone in her household. She was so appreciative of Paul that she opened up to her home to him.

There are people all around you who are looking for encouragement, words of hope, and meaningful relationships. Sometimes we can't see that in others because of our own hangups. Maybe we are upset because life took a turn we didn't plan on. Whatever the reason, the circumstances you find yourself in are not always about you and your personal goals. There might be a bigger reason God has you where you are. To find out why, strive to use whatever circumstance you are in to bring glory to God.

delight |

Have you been guilty of making others around you miserable just because you feel miserable? Why or why not?

How have you personally seen positive people make an impact on others?

display |

Name someone in your life who needs some encouragement. Think of an action you can take to encourage that person and be a good friend. It doesn't have to be big. It could be something as simple as slowing down and asking how their day is going and then listening. Consider how you can make them feel important today and write one idea below.

As you seek to be an encouragement to others, it will be essential that you keep coming to God for your own personal encouragement and fulfillment. Ask Him to "fill you up" so that you can go and share confidently with others about your relationship with Him. Pray that even if you face rejection, you won't take it personally, but you'll continue to be patient and care for that person.

What's the Hurry?

day 21

OPPOSITION IS EXPECTED

discover|

READ ACTS 16:16-24.

Bringing them before the chief magistrates, they said, "These men are seriously disturbing our city. They are Jews and are promoting customs that are not legal for us as Romans to adopt or practice." The crowd joined in the attack against them, and the chief magistrates stripped off their clothes and ordered them to be beaten with rods. —Acts 16:20-22

Just because God purposely placed Paul in Macedonia didn't mean there would be no opposition. One day while they were ministering in the city, a demon-possessed slave girl who could predict the future confronted Paul and his friends. When Paul casted the demon out of her, it really put a damper on her owner's earnings. They wanted him to pay for their loss of income, so they took Paul to the government authorities and made false accusations. Paul took a severe beating for his faith and was thrown into prison.

It's hard to compare the opposition we might face for our faith to Paul's. However, the severity of the opposition Paul faced doesn't downplay the opposition you may face today. There are countless people, cultural messages, and personal insecurities that may discourage you and seek to stop you from continuing in your faith.

Opposition comes in so many forms, and it is important to not compare your struggle with someone else's. However, you are to continually seek to honor God in whatever you are doing. Paul revealed a beatiful model of how to persevere and endure when facing oppostion. He never gave up or lost hope.

delight |

What kind of opposition to your faith do you face everyday?

How might your attitude toward opposition change if you expected it instead of being surprised by it?

display |

Identify some opposition you face in sharing your faith with others. Think through the consequences of remaining silent and decide to take a risk to share anyway. Write out a plan of how you will respond the next time you face oppostion for your belief in Christ.

Pray for confidence in your faith. Ask God to guard you against any opposition that would cause you to lose your faith. Pray that you are strengthened in the midst of your opposition and not frightened.

day 22

GOD DELIVERS

discover |

READ ACTS 16:25-34.

About midnight Paul and Silas were praying and singing hymns to God, and the prisoners were listening to them. —Acts 16:25

After being humiliated and beaten in public for proclaiming their faith, Paul and Silas were put in jail. They were the kind of men who were not deterred by adversity. They were not giving up in their journey to spread the news of Jesus to everyone they encountered. The Bible says that even while they were in jail, they were praying and singing hymns to God—and the other prisoners were listening.

God sent a violent earthquake that shook the jail—all the prison doors opened, and the prisoners' chains were loosened. God came through for His people once again. He provided an escape when things looked bleak.

The Philippian jailer was about to take his own life, thinking his prisoners had escaped. But Paul always sought to save as many people as possible. Even though the doors were opened and his chains were loosened, Paul stayed, talked the jailer out of suicide, and told him about Jesus.

In Romans 12:12, Paul gave advice to others about what to do in tough times. He said to "be patient in affliction." Paul demonstrated in that Philippian jail what patience looks like— trusting and praising God no matter what. He knew every situation he found himself in was ordained by God. He was where God wanted him, and he took that time to share Jesus with others.

delight |

How can you show more patience to others when you are feeling impatient?

How does knowing that God is taking care of you help you to have more patience with others?

display |

When you feel like being impatient, pause a moment. Consider how you can value others when you feel like moving on to the next thing or being somewhere else. Take time to say, "I'm about to go do something else, but before I do, is there anything you need from me?" If you make a practice of asking these kinds of questions, you will be surprised how much the attitudes of the people around you will soften and relax.

Ask God to help you value people over your own agenda. Ask Him to teach you how to be patient with others when you'd rather be doing something else. Thank Him that He took the time with you to hear your prayers and be there for you.

Now to him who is able to do above and beyond all that we ask or think according to the power that works in us—

to him be glory in the church
and in Christ Jesus
to all generations,
forever
and ever.

Amen.

PHESIANS 3:20-21

day 23

PRAYER

discover |

READ PHILIPPIANS 4:6.

Don't worry about anything, but in everything, through prayer and petition with thanksgiving, present your requests to God.

After Paul's arrest, beating, and imprisonment, a group of Philippian believers worshiped together in a local church that Paul planted. It is to this church that Paul wrote these words. He expressed his care for the people and his desire to see them firmly rooted in Jesus.

To worry is to "allow one's mind to dwell on difficulties and troubles."[4] You may think worrying is not a choice. Anxious thoughts just seem to pop in your head automatically. However, the choice to continue to focus and dwell on that thought is yours. Worry is what sticks around when you don't stop your anxious or negative thoughts.

The answer for worry is prayer. Talk to someone who can actually help with what you are worried about. Jesus said, "Come to me, all of you who are weary and burdened, and I will give you rest" (Matt. 11:28). He can help with whatever you are going through. His help may not be what you expected, but He promises to never leave you, and in the end, you won't be disappointed (Heb. 13:5, Rom. 10:11). When you allow your worrisome thoughts to remain, you are choosing to make yourself unhappy. Your Heavenly Father wants to help you. He wants you to bring your concerns to Him. It's for your happiness and His glory when you do.

delight |

What are some worrisome thoughts you struggle with?

How can you develop a habit of turning worries over to God in your daily prayer life?

display |

When you have a worrisome thought, talk to yourself. Say "stop" either in your mind or out loud. Try speaking truth from God's Word to your fears and anxieties. Then, take that same worrisome thought and make it a prayer. Keep up this ritual of saying "stop" and turning the thought into a prayer until it becomes a habit.

Confess your worrisome tendencies. Thank God that He wants to care for you and that He listens to your concerns. Praise Him that He is faithful to guide you.

day 24

SLOW TO SPEAK

discover |

READ JAMES 1:19-21.

My dear brothers and sisters, understand this: Everyone should be quick to listen, slow to speak, and slow to anger, for human anger does not accomplish God's righteousness. —James 1:19-20

James' advice to his readers was that they should be "quick to listen, slow to speak and slow to anger." We all like to feel heard. We all want someone to think about their response before they speak, and we don't want others to rush to anger after we have expressed our thoughts and opinions.

For the follower of Jesus, your anger is not going to accomplish the change of heart in a person that only God can bring about. People may stop a behavior if you get angry with them, but heart change (which is what God is all about) happens through the Holy Spirit.

Proverbs 15:1 says, "A gentle answer turns away anger, but a harsh word stirs up wrath." Your anger with someone will not bring you closer. It will only stir up harsh feelings. Every relationship has tense times when conflict arises. It is only when we reconcile and apologize that relationships are strengthened—not when we yell, name call, or assume the worst about others. Leaving conversations with both parties angry can lead to bitterness and resentment that can last years. A simple apology after a fight can go a long way toward building the kind of friendships that can endure a lifetime.

delight |

How do you like to be treated by others? Do you feel less quick to become angry when the person you are talking to is quick to listen?

How do you usually handle conflict? Are you able to listen and talk calmly without letting your anger take control?

display |

Arguments are inevitable, and although it is better not to lose your temper in the first place, it happens. Is there someone you need to go and apologize to for losing your temper? Go and apologize to him or her. Do your part to repair the relationship as best you can, and if you can't, give them some space and try again later.

Thank God that He is quick to listen, slow to speak, and slow to anger. Ask Him to help you to be like Him in your quickness to listen, slowness to speak, and slowness to anger.

What's the Hurry?

day 25

A SIGN OF COMMITMENT

discover |

READ HEBREWS 6:13-20.

And so, after waiting patiently, Abraham obtained the promise.
—Hebrews 6:15

The writer of Hebrews was concerned for those who might be tempted to leave the faith. He told the people to hold on to the promises of God. The ones who remain faithful and patient receive the rewards God offers (Heb. 6:12). He then gave an example of someone who embodied this truth—Abraham.

God made a great promise to Abraham in Genesis 15 that Abraham's offspring would be as numerous as the stars. God revealed the permanence of His commitment to this promise by having Abraham cut animals in half. God then passed through the animal halves.

It may seem like an odd ceremony for us today for someone to pass through slaughtered animals as a sign of commitment, but it meant something very significant back then. Whoever walked through the animal halves was saying, "If I break my promise to you, may I be like these animals." It was a very serious commitment, and God meant every bit of it. Abraham believed God, and the Bible says God counted his belief as righteousness.

What is your sign that God is committed to His promises to you? It is His Son, Jesus. Jesus' death and resurrection is the evidence that God will also conquer death in you and you will live forever with Him. The question for you is, "Will you trust this promise?"

delight |

Do you have a hard time believing that other people will keep their promises to you? Why or why not?

What are some of the promises you have read about in Scripture that God has made to you?

display |

Look at your list of Scriptural promises you wrote down. Reflect on how you would think and behave differently if you truly believed these promises were true every moment of your life. Start believing and adopt thoughts and behaviors that reflect the reality of these truths today. Write down one way you will put this into practice today.

Claim God's promises for yourself. In your prayers, remind God of His promises to you. God is not forgetful, but He does appreciate you speaking His Words back to Him. Thank Him for Jesus' death and resurrection as His symbol of promise to you.

day 26

THE BATTLE IS THE LORD'S

discover |

READ EXODUS 14:5-14.

But Moses said to the people, "Don't be afraid. Stand firm and see the Lord's salvation that he will accomplish for you today; for the Egyptians you see today, you will never see again. The Lord will fight for you, and you must be quiet."
—Exodus 14:13-14

The Israelite people had been enslaved by the Egyptians for over 400 years. These people didn't even know a life apart from slavery. They had been crying out to God to rescue them for years. The Egyptians were cruel taskmasters, and God's people suffered under them. Finally, God sent Moses to rescue the people out of Egypt. God sent plagues that destroyed the Egyptian water, land, animals, and people until Pharaoh released the Israelites.

As they were leaving, Pharaoh changed his mind and wanted the people back. He gathered an army of hundreds of men and chariots and rode after the Israelites. Understandably, the Israelites panicked. They blamed Moses and began to wonder if an enslaved life might have been better. All the while, God never left them. He was still fighting their battles for them. All He asked of His people was to trust Him to deliver them.

Jesus told His disciples just before His arrest, "You will have suffering in this world. Be courageous! I have conquered the world" (John 16:33). Jesus has guaranteed us victory through Him. We just have to trust in Him. We just need to quiet our worries and believe His Word is true.

delight |

How does panic show up in your behaviors?

How can knowing that God has everything under His control help you handle situations that might cause you to panic?

display |

Memorize Ephesians 3:20-21. When you are about to panic, force yourself to repeat these verses to yourself over and over. Remind yourself that this world is not all there is to your life and that you serve a powerful God who fights on your side.

Praise God for fighting your battle of sin and death through His Son, Jesus. Spend time asking Him to calm your fears and give you rest for your soul.

While You Wait

God doesn't operate on our timetable because He exists and works outside of time as we know it. So, it can seem like we spend a lot of time waiting for God to move. In reality, He's preparing us for what's to come in His perfect timing.

The Bible is full of examples of godly men and women who spent a lot of time waiting. Some waited their entire lives to see a promise come to fruition, and others were patient even without seeing any "proof." Look at the list of names and Scripture passages on the left and draw a line to match them with how the person revealed patience while waiting on the Lord.

Abraham and Sarah
(Gen. 12:1-3; 18:9-15; 21:2-4)

Joseph
(Gen. 37:5-11,27-28; 45; 50)

Job
(Job 1:22; Jas. 5:11)

Zechariah and Elizabeth
(Luke 1:5-25; 57-66)

Simeon
(Luke 2:25-35)

Paul
*(Acts 16:16-25;
21:26-36; 28:30-31)*

He was 100 years old when his son was born. His wife laughed when God told her she would have a child.

She was barren, and they were both "well along in years." When an angel told him they would have a son, he didn't believe it, so he couldn't speak until his son was born.

The Holy Spirit revealed to this man that he wouldn't die until he got to meet the Messiah. He spoke prophetic words over Jesus.

This man was imprisoned twice, but continued his ministry even in chains.

His brothers sold him into slavery and he was wrongfully imprisoned. But God raised him up to be the Pharaoh's right hand man, and his wisdom spared many during a famine.

He lost everything he owned, along with His children. Yet, he refused to accuse God for his trials.

While each of these men and women waited for God to fulfill His promises to them or waited on the Lord to move them out of heartbreaking circumstances, we see one key factor over and over: God was with them in the waiting. He met each one of them right where they were, and He does the same for us.

We may not ever see the result of our efforts, the resolution to a certain issue, or healing in a specific relationship, but we can wholeheartedly trust that God is moving and working in our lives whether we see His hand actively or not.

In fact, take a look at Hebrews 11. If you write in your Bible or use a Bible app, highlight every time you see the words "by faith." In the Christian Standard Bible, the phrase occurs 22 times in this passage! These men and women were patience pros. They lived their lives fully and vibrantly for the Lord, all without seeing the promise completely fulfilled in Jesus.

By faith, will you trust God, too?

Spend some time reflecting in prayer. In what area of life are you struggling to be patient or wait on the Lord to move? Journal your response.

day 27

FLEE FROM EVIL

discover |

READ 2 TIMOTHY 3:1-9.

People will be lovers of self, lovers of money, boastful, proud, demeaning, disobedient to parents, ungrateful, unholy, unloving, irreconcilable, slanderers, without self-control, brutal, without love for what is good, traitors, reckless, conceited, lovers of pleasure rather than lovers of God, holding to the form of godliness but denying its power. Avoid these people. —2 Timothy 3:2-5

The apostle Paul wrote this letter to his "spiritual son" Timothy. Paul had discipled Timothy and given him a place of leadership in a church he started. Paul wrote this letter to help Timothy be prepared for what circumstances were going to look like as they waited for Jesus' return.

The description of people's behaviors in the last days wasn't pretty. These characteristics describe someone who has chosen to serve himself or herself over God. They have traded in serving the God who sent His only Son to reconcile all people to Himself for momentary pleasure and self-gratification.

There are several lists throughout Scripture of the characteristics of a genuine believer in Christ. Galatians 5:22-23 is one such passage: "the fruit of the Spirit is love, joy, peace, patience, kindness, goodness, faithfulness, gentleness, and self-control." These are the characteristics we are to chase after. They are characteristics that honor God, show His nature to the world, and honor others as valuable. Someone who has these traits builds authentic relationships with others and glorifies God with his or her life.

delight |

As you read over 2 Timothy 3:2-5, do you feel convicted about any of those characteristics for yourself?

Why do you think it would be a good idea to not be surrounded by people who practice these kinds of behaviors?

display |

You may feel you are not measuring up to the descriptions of a Christian and that your life sounds more like the description of a person the Bible says to avoid. Don't be discouraged! Sometimes in the process of becoming more like Christ, we see our sin more clearly, and it feels like we are failing when actually we are making real progress. So, rejoice that you want to make a change, and keep going!

Praise God that He doesn't leave you as you are, but that He is continually working on your character. Ask Him to help you make tough decisions about the people you allow to influence your life. Pray that He would keep you on the path to growing to be more like Jesus.

day 28

FOLLOWING IN PATIENCE

discover |

READ 2 TIMOTHY 3:10-13.

But you have followed my teaching, conduct, purpose, faith, patience, love, and endurance. —2 Timothy 3:10

In these verses, Paul commended Timothy for following his example. Timothy showed himself to be a faithful friend and dedicated disciple. Paul met Timothy on one of his missionary journeys. Fellow believers told Paul what a great person Timothy was, and Paul found their reports to be true (Acts 16:2). After meeting TImothy, Paul decided to take him along on his other journeys, and they worked together to instruct numerous others in the way of Jesus.

But Paul was not Timothy's first mentor. Timothy's mother and grandmother were also believers. We don't have a lot of details about these women, but Paul called their faith sincere (2 Tim. 3:5). Timothy's faith and conduct was marked and shaped by the examples he chose to spend his life following—Paul, his mother and his grandmother.

It is the example of others we choose to follow that will mold our character. Timothy was able to grow by following the examples before him. Paul is not here today for us to follow, but he and other faithful people have left writings to encourage us and inspire us to follow their teaching, conduct, faith, love, endurance, and patience.

delight |

How could being around a patient person help you to be patient with others?

Other than following an example of someone you know personally, what are other ways you can find examples for you to grow your character?

display |

As you think about who you follow (and not just on social media), consider their influence on you. Decide the person you want to be in five years, ten years, and twenty years. Start surrounding yourself with people who will help you on that path. Also, be aware of relationships in which you are a positive influence. Make an effort to be the kind of person you want others to look up to. Write the name of one person whose faith you would like to imitate.

If you already have a spiritual mentor, thank God for that person. If you don't, ask God to bring one into your life. Also ask God to show you someone you can be an example of godliness to.

day 29

THE POWER OF GOD'S WORD

discover |

READ 2 TIMOTHY 3:14-17.

All Scripture is inspired by God and is profitable for teaching, for rebuking, for correcting, for training in righteousness, so that the man of God may be complete, equipped for every good work. —2 Timothy 3:16-17

There is power in the words of God. Power to give life, power to heal, and power to reveal the very intentions of our hearts (Heb. 4:12). We are able to get a better picture of our desires, thoughts, and wants as we read the Word. It will show you the patterns in your life that are hindering you from what God has for you and the patterns that will give you abundant life.

Paul told Timothy that the Scriptures are profitable for teaching, rebuking, correcting, and training in righteousness. All of these words lend themselves to images of a person coaching another. God's Word is like your personal trainer for spiritual fitness. It tells you the exercises to prepare for God's work in your sphere of influence.

When you are seeking to be more patient with yourself and with others, let the Word be your guide. You will find encouragement to keep pursuing patience, examples of others who modeled patience, and words of warning against impatience. If God's words are powerful enough to create the world and bring the dead to life, they can certainly change a stubborn heart into a patient and loving one.

delight |

Share a time when someone's words had a powerful impact on you. How so?

Do you believe in the power of God's Word? Why or why not?

display |

You are almost finished with this exploration in patience. Spend some time finding your next devotion. Commit to studying your Bible everyday for the next 30 days. As you study, journal thoughts as you have them and changes that you observe the Lord bringing about in yourself.

Thank God that He left you His words in the Bible. Pray that He will transform you to the image of His Son as you study His Word.

day 30

███████ ──

discover |

READ PSALM 37:7-9.

Be silent before the Lord and wait expectantly for him; do not be agitated by one who prospers in his way, by the person who carries out evil plans. Refrain from anger and give up your rage; do not be agitated—it can only bring harm. For evildoers will be destroyed, but those who put their hope in the Lord will inherit the land.

The great King David of Israel wrote these words to encourage others to maintain their hope in God. One of their biggest distractions (and probably yours, too) from waiting on God was when they saw someone else prosper. When we see others doing well who we know are not waiting on God, it makes us want to quit what we are doing and go after what others have.

His advice is to "wait expectantly for him." To wait expectantly means you trust God to do something. It is not the kind of waiting that waves a white flag and accepts a life of disappointments. It's the kind of waiting that is optimistic that your situation is only temporary and that things will change in time. It's the kind of waiting that builds your relationship with God—not the opposite.

The bottom line is that you will need to exercise patience when others prosper while you don't, but your patience is grounded in a God who cares for you. He wants you to succeed. He wants you to achieve great things, but they will only come about through His ways and His timing. Only those who maintain hope will receive the promised rewards.

delight |

Describe a time when you felt you deserved what someone else had.

What became of your feelings? Did it hurt your relationship with that person or with God?

display |

Read Romans 8:31-39. Journal about how you know God wants the best for you. (Hint: the answer is in verses 31-32). Also, take note about what will separate you from the love of God. Write how being reassured of God's goodness and love can help you wait on Him.

> Confess times when you grew angry over others' success. Bring any concerns of your own failure to God. Ask for His help to remain faithful to Him while you wait.

In Pursuit of Patience:

Six Steps to Help You Overcome Irritation and Choose Love

Breathe.

When you find yourself feeling impatient with a person or situation, remember to breathe. Sometimes we're tempted to hold our breath until resolution comes, but that is neither healthy nor recommended. Taking a deep breath in and slowly exhaling can actually slow your heart rate from its irritated pitter-patter to a normal rhythm.

This would also be a good moment to pray for patience. Despite what we might think, asking God for patience shouldn't be some flippant request of "Lord, help me not to go off on this person!" Praying for patience focuses on your heart being right before God. Ask Him to soften your heart toward Him and others, then ask Him to help you continue to grow in His likeness—including having His heart for patience.

Retreat.

Remember this: You're human, and you won't get it right every time. But with God's help, you can handle more than you might think. You can have extraordinary patience. By listening to the Holy Spirit's guidance, you might determine that the best course of action is to retreat. This doesn't mean that you never address the issue; it simply means you're taking a step back from the moment to refocus on the big picture. When we have the opportunity to remove ourselves from a stressful situation, we can often return to the conversation later with a clear head and calm heart.

Perceive.

Whether you're breathing or retreating, take a good look at your perception of the person or event. In the moment, we tend to respond emotionally to stressful situations, maybe as a result of feeling attacked or because our stress level is already seriously high. When someone does something that offends you or accuses you of hurting them, tap into your perception of events. Try to look at the situation as an outsider and ask yourself some key questions:

- What am I currently going through that might be coloring my perception?
- Is there any truth to the accusation? If so, how can I address this issue in a godly way, even if I don't appreciate the way it was presented?
- If there's no truth to the accusation, ask yourself: What might he/she be going through that could make him/her feel stressed/anxious/angry?

Set Your Mind and Focus Your Heart.

Our mindsets and the focus of our hearts greatly affect our response to difficult situations. If we want to respond in God-honoring, Christ-centered ways, then our minds need to be set on His Word and our hearts need to be focused on Him. Even in the middle of tough situations, we can't lose sight of the One who matters more than everything and loves us all more than anything.

Praying for patience is often reduced to a humorous quip or caution not to pray for patience as if God would punish you by then making you wait. Here's the truth: Things were always going to happen in God's timing, and they always will. So, don't be afraid to pray for patience. While part of praying for patience is getting your own heart right before God, we also need to remember who it is we're praying to. Approach God with praise for His character and thank Him for the way He loves us. When you've done these two things, your heart is in the right place to pray for the other person.

Respond.
If you need to retreat from a situation, be sure to communicate your heart plainly to the other person. You might say something like, "Thanks for coming to me about this, _____ (name). I know that wasn't easy. I want to honor you in my response, so I'd like some time to think over what you've said."

If it seems that he or she is just having an off day or there's something going on, perceive the mood in the room (asking the Holy Spirit for guidance here is key). Consider asking: "Hey, _____ (name), it sounds like you're having a tough day. How can I help?" If he or she is a believer, offer to pray together.

Only God knows the motives of our hearts, so we might not understand why people do what they do, but we don't have to. God calls us to love as He loves us (John 13:34), and sometimes the most loving response we can have is to say and do nothing—refuse to fuel the fire anger feeds. Remember that no response is a response, too.

Trust God.
No matter what the situation or how well or imperfectly you handled things, trust God with the outcome. We cannot control anyone's response but our own, and we can only do that through the presence and guidance of the Holy Spirit. Trust that God loves you and this other person immensely, and regardless of what it might seem like in the moment, He cares so much about what you're going through. Throughout Scripture, we see His faithfulness, kindness, goodness, and love for people. We can trust that He has everyone's best interests at heart.

Challenge: Commit to implementing these steps next time you have a conflict with someone. In a journal or notebook, write about that experience. Then, write out a prayer for that person.

What's the Hurry?

Notes

Notes

Endnotes

1. BookBrowse, "Why Do We Say Patience Is a Virtue?," BookBrowse.com, accessed March 26, 2021, https://www.bookbrowse.com/expressions/detail/index.cfm/expression_number/416/patience-is-a-virtue.

2. Erik Gregersen. "History of Technology Timeline." Encyclopædia Britannica. Encyclopædia Britannica, inc. Accessed March 26, 2021. https://www.britannica.com/story/history-of-technology-timeline.

3. Trevin Wax, "C.S. Lewis on Life's Interruptions," The Gospel Coalition, February 26, 2011, https://www.thegospelcoalition.org/blogs/trevin-wax/c-s-lewis-on-lifes-interruptions/.

4. "Worry," Oxford Dictionary (Lexico), accessed March 26, 2021, https://www.lexico.com/en/definition/worry.